Helen Francis

D1643667

Series 561

THE STORY OF
Sir WALTER RALEIGH

by L. DU GARDE PEACH, M.A., Ph.D., D.Litt.
with illustrations by JOHN KENNEY

Publishers: Wills & Hepworth Ltd., Loughborough
First published 1957   ©   *Printed in England*

SIR WALTER RALEIGH

Four centuries ago, in the year 1558, a young Queen ascended the throne of England. Like our own Queen to-day, her name was Elizabeth, and during her long reign of forty-five years, England enjoyed one of the greatest periods in all our history.

When Elizabeth, a beautiful young woman of twenty-five, rode through the streets of London to her coronation, surrounded by all the brilliant colour and pageantry of the sixteenth century, it must have been one of the most wonderful sights the old city had ever seen.

But England was neither happy nor contented. The reign of Elizabeth's elder sister Mary had nearly caused a revolution at home, and in the war with France, the English had been defeated abroad. There was no money in the treasury, and overseas trade had disappeared.

Many people in the country were starving, and others were still suffering from the cruel persecution of the previous reign.

The roads of England were unsafe because of robbers and homeless outlaws, and throughout the length and breadth of the land, there was neither law nor order, as we know them to-day.

During the reign of Elizabeth all this was changed, and England became prosperous and happy.

Much of this was due to the brave sailors who were known as gentlemen-adventurers. These men, sailing their little ships to the furthest limits of the known oceans, made Elizabethan England the mistress of the seas.

Two of the greatest of them were still boys in Devon when Elizabeth came to the throne. They were Francis Drake, who was fifteen, and his young kinsman, Walter Raleigh, who was six.

When he was twenty, Drake sailed in command of a little ship to the newly discovered continent of America. His object was to win from the Spaniards some of the gold which they had discovered there. He returned with a wonderful story of adventure to tell to his young friend, Walter Raleigh.

As Walter Raleigh listened, he was no doubt thrilled at the thought of one day sailing westward to fight the Spaniards. Day after day he looked out over the sea, and wondered what he would find beyond the horizon.

In the meantime, like most Devon boys, he spent all the time he could on or in the water. The little boats of four hundred years ago were clumsy things compared with the trim yachts of to-day, but young Walter Raleigh and his friends learnt to sail them in all weathers.

Though he did not know it, it was the preparation for those great voyages on which the British Empire has been founded, and which to-day we know as the British Commonwealth of Nations.

A boy of a good family could not spend all his time sailing small boats. Young Walter Raleigh had to be educated to take his proper place in the world.

He was only sixteen when he went to Oriel College, Oxford. Here he found a new interest, equal all through his life with his love of the sea. For the first time he was surrounded by books in great numbers.

Walter Raleigh became one of the scholars of his age. He wrote some very good poetry, as well as a number of books. Later, whilst in prison in the Tower of London, he started to write a history of the world.

But his love of books and of learning did not prevent him from sailing to the Spanish Main in search of adventure, when the time came.

Young Walter Raleigh was eager for adventure on land, as well as at sea. It was only a year after he went to Oxford that he saw service as a soldier in France.

In that country there was a struggle going on between the protestants and the catholics, and many Englishmen went over to help one side or the other. Being a protestant, Raleigh joined the protestant side, known as the Huguenots.

This was not a war between two countries, but the fighting was no less fierce. In fact, because they were fighting about religious differences, it was even more bitter and cruel. There were many battles up and down the country and Raleigh, who had gone with a company of volunteers led by his cousin, fought at the battle of Jarnac, in western France. But the protestants were defeated, and Raleigh came back to his books in England.

When Walter Raleigh was a young man of twenty-six, he made his first voyage to the west. His half-brother, Sir Humphrey Gilbert, had been asked by Queen Elizabeth to sail to the northern part of America, to find some uninhabited part of the country in which people from England could found a colony. He took several ships, and one of them was commanded by Walter Raleigh.

It was a very little ship called the Falcon, not the sort of ship in which anyone would like to sail far to-day. But it was strong and seaworthy, and in it Raleigh and his sailors safely weathered the great storms of the northern ocean.

The voyage was not very successful, but Walter Raleigh learned a great deal about the new world. This helped him later when he made his famous voyages.

In Elizabethan times, the life of a young man was full of all sorts of adventures. Only two years after he had sailed his ship amongst the icebergs and the storms of the north, Walter Raleigh was fighting as a soldier in Ireland.

This was very different from anything which Raleigh had known before. Ireland was a wild country and the fighting was very fierce indeed. But Raleigh was a recklessly brave young man, and fought so well, that he was chosen to go back to England to tell Queen Elizabeth about the battles with the Irish.

It was a long and difficult journey from Ireland to England in those days, but Raleigh was eager to get to the court of Queen Elizabeth, there to make his fortune.

In this Walter Raleigh was right, the Queen loved to be surrounded by handsome young men, and Raleigh was one of the handsomest men of his time. It was an age when men wore clothes of velvet and brocade, with ornaments of gold and many jewels. Raleigh's youthful figure set off these clothes to advantage, and with his trim, pointed beard, and his eager eyes, he must have looked like a hero out of a story book.

He was as gallant as he was good-looking. When Raleigh arrived at the palace, Elizabeth was walking in the grounds, surrounded by her courtiers.

Suddenly the Queen stopped. The path was wet and muddy, and Elizabeth in her golden shoes and silken dress, hesitated to pass. The courtiers did not know what to do, but in an instant Raleigh had swept off his rich velvet cloak, and spread it across the mud at the Queen's feet.

Queen Elizabeth was not likely to over-look a young man who was ready to sacrifice his fine cloak so that she should not get her feet wet. When Raleigh, dressed in a rich brocade doublet, slashed with silk, and a starched white ruff, arrived to present his report he was received with royal favour.

In those days men were rewarded by being given the right to sell something which no one else was allowed to offer. Raleigh was not only granted some of these rights, but he was given a fine house in the Strand and a licence to export woollen cloth.

This cloth was one of the chief things made in England to be sold to people in other countries. As the English merchants were obliged to pay Raleigh a tax on every yard which they sold, he soon became a very rich man.

As Raleigh grew in favour with the Queen, further honours were showered upon him. He was made " Warden of the Stanneries," which meant that he was in control of the tin mines in Devon and Cornwall. Raleigh was a Devon man himself, so he knew all about the miners and was liked by them. He was fair to everybody and they trusted him, and, of course, he was able to make a lot more money out of selling the tin.

Walter Raleigh did not come of a noble family. His father was a simple Devon squire. But now Elizabeth decided to make him a knight, and he became Sir Walter Raleigh.

It must have been a very wonderful scene when Queen Elizabeth, in her gorgeous jewelled robes, with a drawn sword in her hand, touched the shoulder of the young man kneeling before her, and said, " Rise, Sir Walter."

The fighting in Ireland had been against an Irish lord, the Earl of Desmond. When Desmond was beaten, all his lands in the south of Ireland were given to Raleigh by the Queen, and he suddenly found himself one of the greatest landowners of Ireland.

Raleigh later put this land to good use by growing potatoes, the roots of which had been brought back to England by his sailors from Virginia. It is strange to think that there were no potatoes in Britain at all, until Raleigh introduced them.

Another plant which Raleigh brought to England was tobacco. Discovered by the Spaniards in America, it had been used on the continent as a medicine, and it was not until a man called Ralph Lane, the first Governor of Virginia, told Raleigh that the red indians used it for smoking, that the habit came to Europe. Before then, no one had smoked at all, and when Raleigh's servant first saw him smoking a pipe of tobacco, he thought he was on fire, and threw a bucket of water over him.

You will remember that when Raleigh was a young man of twenty-six he had sailed to America with Sir Humphrey Gilbert. The Queen had given Sir Humphrey a document, authorising him to occupy uninhabited lands.

Now that Sir Humphrey Gilbert had died, Raleigh asked the Queen to transfer to him the right to look for new lands in the west, and Elizabeth was graciously pleased to renew what was called the " patent."

Of course, in those days, not many people had been to North America, and it was inhabited only by a few tribes of red indians. But Raleigh saw that it was good land, the sort of country in which Englishmen could plant farms and make a good living.

The Queen was very interested when he showed her the maps and charts, and he promised to name the new land Virginia in her honour. One of the United States of America is still called Virginia to this day.

Raleigh did not sail on this voyage to the west. He had been made the Captain of the Queen's Guard, and had to stay in England.

So he did what other rich men did at that time: he fitted out two ships and sent them to find the new lands across the sea.

Although he did not sail himself with the ships, we can be sure that he carefully watched their fitting out, because he knew all the things that would be needed on such a voyage. His two captains, who were called Philip Amadas and Arthur Barlowe, would be with him day after day, studying the charts and going over the lists of stores.

It would be a brave sight when the two ships sailed, dressed overall with flags, and there would be trumpets and the firing of cannon. Raleigh, as he stood on the quay and watched them, probably wished that he, too, were going.

Other events kept Raleigh in England besides his duties at the palace. In this same year he became the Member of Parliament for Devonshire.

This may seem a strange thing for a man to do, who had spent all his life either as a soldier or a sailor. But Raleigh was now Sir Walter Raleigh, well known and a great landowner, and in those days it was the duty of such men to go into Parliament.

This was long before ordinary people voted for Members of Parliament, as they do to-day, and the House of Commons did not have anything like as much power as it has now. If the Queen did not like anything the Members did, she simply sent them away and ruled without them.

Raleigh was now thirty-two years old, and when he made a speech in the House of Commons, it must have looked something like this picture.

When Raleigh's two captains came back from their voyage with wonderful stories of the rich land they had found, Raleigh and his friends decided to send some men to make farms and start a colony.

This time there were seven small ships, commanded by the famous Sir Richard Grenville, who was Raleigh's cousin. On board the ships there were more than 100 men, with all the things which they would need to start their farms.

In April they sailed from Plymouth, and four months later they landed on Roanoke Island, a part of the State now called North Carolina.

Soon the men were hard at work, chopping down trees and building their farm houses. Then they had to clear the land and plant their crops.

It was not long before they were visited by the red indians who lived in the country, and for a time they were all quite friendly.

Unfortunately things went wrong with the little colony on Roanoke Island. The crops did not come up, perhaps because they were the wrong sort of seeds, or because some of the men did not know much about farming.

This was a serious matter for the colonists. The failure of the crops meant that they had no corn to make bread, and soon they knew that unless ships came from England, they would starve.

But this was not the worst thing that happened to them. The red indians, who had been so friendly to start with, did not like it when they found that the white men had come to take away their land. So the colonists had to spend most of their time defending themselves against the red indians, and they were very glad when some ships, commanded by the famous Sir Francis Drake, came to take them away.

Whilst all this was happening over in the new lands of America, Raleigh was receiving fresh honours at home. One of these was his appointment as Vice-Admiral of Devon.

In those days most of the sailors who manned the English ships came from the West Country. Little places like Lyme Regis and Sidmouth, Topsham and Dartmouth, Fowey and Falmouth, were as important as Plymouth is to-day. In all of them ships were built, and from all of them these ships were soon to sail to keep England free.

So it was very important that a man who knew all about ships and the sea, and who was also a brave fighting man, should be in command of the West Country ports.

No better man than Sir Walter Raleigh could have been chosen. He was young, handsome, popular, and a Devon man known and respected by everyone.

Soon the time came when every sailor and every ship were needed for the defence of England against the great Armada of Spain.

Philip of Spain was at that time the most powerful king in Europe, and he very much wanted to add England to his possessions. There were a lot of reasons for this. One of them was because Englishmen like Raleigh and Drake and Richard Grenville were stopping and capturing the treasure ships which sailed from America to Spain.

So Philip gathered together a fleet of 130 ships with more than 20,000 men. They set sail from Lisbon in May, but it was not until the middle of July that they appeared off Plymouth.

This fleet was called the Armada, and when its sails appeared far out to sea, Drake and Raleigh and the other English captains were playing bowls on Plymouth Hoe.

Some of them wanted to sail at once to meet the enemy, but Drake said, " There is time to finish our game and beat the Spaniards, too." So the game went on.

When the game was finished, the English fleet sailed out of Plymouth harbour. There were about 190 English ships, but most of them were very small, no bigger than the little boats which to-day we call yachts.

The big Spanish ships sailed up the Channel with the English attacking them whenever they could. Finally, the Spaniards anchored in Calais harbour, where they thought they were safe.

But the English captains had another idea. They set some of their own ships on fire, and sent them into the harbour amongst the Spanish ships. This so frightened the Spaniards that they tried to put to sea again, but stormy weather drove them far to the north, and only half of them ever got back to Spain.

Raleigh returned to England and to a life full of adventure. He took part in an invasion of Portugal and made several voyages to capture Spanish treasure ships. For Raleigh was before all things a sailor, and always, whatever he was doing, he longed to get back to the sea.

His chance came again when everyone was talking about El Dorado—which means the golden country. People thought that there were whole mountains of solid gold in South America, and Raleigh decided to go and see for himself. He knew that this would probably mean fighting with the Spaniards, but at that time this was something which every Englishman wanted to do.

So again Raleigh sailed to the west. He did not find the mountains of gold, but he landed on the Island of Trinidad, which then belonged to Spain, and captured and burnt the town of San Jose de Oruna.

Since the Armada, England had always been more or less at war with Spain. From time to time English ships sailed out to attack Spanish towns or Spanish ships, and it was during one of these sorties that Raleigh was wounded.

The Spanish town of Cadiz, not very far from the straits of Gibraltar, was one of the richest cities in the world, because all the gold and silver from South America was brought there by the Spanish galleons. This was just the sort of place which attracted the sailors of the Elizabethan age.

Cadiz had been attacked by Drake only two years before. He had burned all the ships in the harbour, but he had not captured the town. So when the Earl of Essex and Lord Charles Howard got together ships to attack Cadiz, Raleigh went with them.

In the attack Raleigh was badly wounded, and had to be carried to the ships by his men.

It was also in the reign of Elizabeth that William Shakespeare lived.

Shakespeare was the greatest poet and writer of plays the world has ever known, and his plays were all produced in a strange sort of theatre on the south bank of the Thames, in London. Walter Raleigh must often have visited this theatre.

But it was not at all like the theatres we visit to-day. To begin with, it had no roof, because there was no electric light, and the plays were acted by daylight. The stage, too, looked very different from the stage of a pantomime or play to-day, because there was no scenery. The actors came out on to a platform, right in the middle of the audience, to play their parts and sing their songs.

The picture shows the play of Hamlet, the greatest of all Shakespeare's plays, as it was first played, in the Globe Theatre.

When Queen Elizabeth died, and James I became King of England, Raleigh lost a friend and gained an enemy.

James wanted to be at peace with Spain, and in order to gain Philip's friendship, he took away from Raleigh all the things which Elizabeth had given him. But Philip, who, of course, hated Raleigh because he had captured so many Spanish ships and taken so many Spanish towns, was not satisfied. He wanted James to have Raleigh executed.

King James would not go so far as this, but he had Raleigh arrested and put in the Tower of London. He was to remain there for fifteen years, except for one more voyage to the west. He was allowed out of the Tower to go on this voyage because he promised King James that he would bring back a ship full of gold. When he failed to do this, James was more angry with him than ever.

Our last picture is of Walter Raleigh in the Tower of London.

He was not kept locked up in a cell, or put into a dark dungeon, as so many prisoners were in those days. He had pleasant rooms, and could do what he liked, but he was not allowed to go outside the Tower walls.

To occupy his time, Raleigh wrote verses and books. One of these was the first volume of a History of the World.

Another of his ways of filling up the long days was to make experiments in chemistry.

In an age of great men—soldiers, sailors, explorers, scholars, and poets—Walter Raleigh stands amongst the greatest. He had in himself something of all of them, and whenever we think of the age of Elizabeth, we think of the gallant gentleman-adventurer who founded the beginnings of the British Empire.

Series 561